ARCHITECTURE & DESIGN LIBRARY

MEDITERRANEAN STYLE

ARCHITECTURE & DESIGN LIBRARY

MEDITERRANEAN STYLE

Robert Fitzgerald

FRIEDMAN/FAIRFAX
PUBLISHERS

A FRIEDMAN/FAIRFAX BOOK
Please visit our website: www.metrobooks.com

Library of Congress Cataloging-in-Publication data available upon request.

ISBN 1-56799-765-1

Editor: Reka Simonsen
Art Director: Jeff Batzli
Designer: Jennifer Markson
Photography Editor: Wendy Missan
Production Director: Karen Matsu Greenberg

Color separations by Colourscan Overseas Pte Ltd.
Printed in Hong Kong by Midas Printing Limited

3 5 7 9 10 8 6 4 2

Distributed by Sterling Publishing Company, Inc.
387 Park Avenue South
New York, NY 10016
Distributed in Canada by Sterling Publishing
Canadian Manda Group
One Atlantic Avenue, Suite 105
Toronto, Ontario, Canada M6K 3E7
Distributed in Australia by
Capricorn Link (Australia) Pty Ltd.
P.O. Box 6651
Baulkham Hills, Business Centre, NSW 2153, Australia

To Ilaria

Contents

INTRODUCTION

Few places on earth stir the imagination like the islands and coastal regions of the Mediterranean. A mental tour of the area evokes powerful, mystical images of land and sea: from the fishing villages of the Costa Brava to the lofty ridges and deep ravines of Mallorca's serra; eastward across the French garriguette to the vaunted beaches and lively ports of the Côte d'Azur and the Italian Riviera; down along the rocky cliffs of the Amalfi Coast and across to the distant outposts of Sicily, Sardinia, and the fragrant Corsican maquis; through the ancient Aegean waters of Greece and the sun-drenched Cyclades; down the coast of Persia and westward again across the mountains and hot desert sands of Tunisia and Morocco. The mind seems to travel to the distant corners of the world but in fact covers just over two thousand miles (3,218km) on this brief journey before doubling back along the coast of Africa.

The Mediterranean's small physical stature, however, belies its enormous historical and cultural influence. For a long while, the Mediterranean existed as a world unto itself. The cradles of Judaism, Christianity, and Islam were are all founded on the Mediterranean's eastern shores. The birthplace of Western civilization, the Mediterranean has also been the battleground of history's great empires, from the ancient Phoenicians and Carthaginians to the Persians, Greeks, Romans, Byzantines, Moors, and Ottomans. Through the present day, the Mediterranean has been an essential conduit for trade and commerce and has been the strategic keystone of every European military effort, including both world wars.

History is palpable in the Mediterranean region. Nature itself appears old and wizened. The terrain looks like an archaeological ruin, splintered and broken. The sun is a constant blazing sentinel. Even the water feels ancient. Virtually landlocked, the Mediterranean Sea seems to contain the history of the region, each handful of water reflecting the stories of countless lives on the sea. Lapping against the wrinkled coast, the sea rises and falls like a metronome, constantly marking the passage of time.

OPPOSITE: *Twilight on the Mediterranean comes in infinite, ever-changing colors and passions. No two sunsets are ever the same, and the texture and intensity of the sky and sea vary greatly according to time and place.*

The sea has been shared by the various Mediterranean peoples for centuries; it is the theme of life in the region. It provides a spiritual connection that is beyond the realm of language, race, and nationality, and imbues the land with a powerful sense of history. Tradition is strong, and Mediterraneans along the rural coastline live today much as their families did many generations ago. The sea still represents a way of life, a livelihood, and a nourishing life force. Watching a fleet of fishing boats leave the harbor, one suspects that the scene would have been much the same a century ago. It is not hard to imagine young Odysseus setting sail to explore the far reaches of the world. Such is the mysterious vastness of the Mediterranean even today.

Life on the Mediterranean is slow and relaxed. Days are long, and the pace of life is ruled by age-old rituals. Mealtimes are sacred, and the afternoon siesta brings the region to a standstill. Simple pleasures are savored: the soft light of the morning sun; a favorite view of the sea; the smell of wildflowers and herbs along a roadside; the spectacle of fishermen returning to port with brimming, quivering nets; the lingering warmth of sand after the sun has faded. The Mediterranean awakens the senses to the nuances of the passing day.

These simple pleasures are translated into home design. The Mediterranean house is a sensual domain, one that piques and coddles the senses much like the surrounding countryside. The home is a medley of colors, textures, and scents that nurture the senses and makes one feel vital and alive. Domestic life and particularly home design play an essential role in conveying the essence of Mediterranean life.

While there is no single look that embodies the countless architectural idiosyncrasies of Mediterranean culture, there are certain design tendencies that can be distilled and considered elements of Mediterranean style. Nature and history, culture, lifestyle, and an acute sense of awareness all come together to make the Mediterranean home a place of astounding beauty.

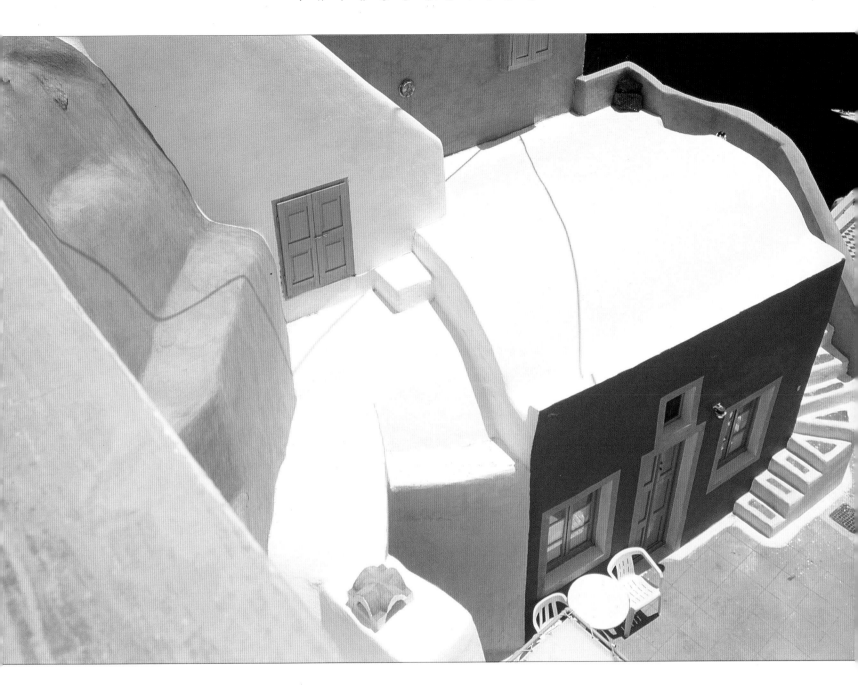

ABOVE: *But for its vivid colors, this home on the island of Thira in the Greek Cyclades would look as if it had been carved out of the side of a mountain. Stucco lends itself to fluid, naturalistic forms such as this. The azure blue and white color scheme is a hallmark of Greek design.*

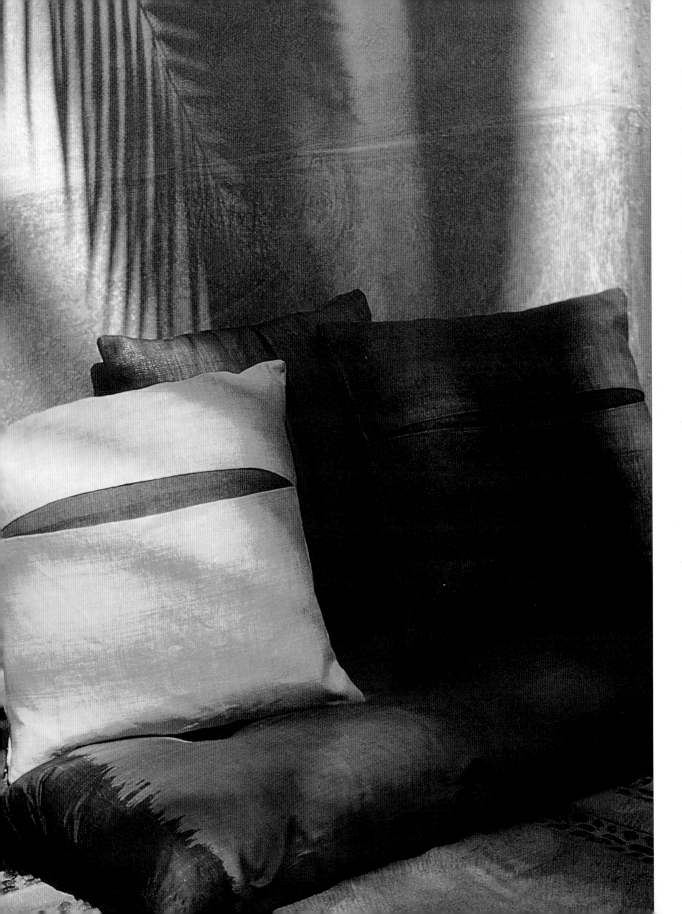

LEFT:

*Mediterranean design
and architecture
are as relaxed and
uncomplicated as
the lifestyle. A few
colorful pillows and
the shade of some
palm fronds make
a perfect settee just
about anywhere.
Pillows covered in
thick, durable fabric
can be placed on the
floor or even outside
in the garden for an
impromptu picnic or
bottle of wine.*

RIGHT:

In northern Africa, houses tend to have thick walls with small windows and doors that help insulate against the heat. Thus, interiors such as this Moroccan bedroom often look like sculpted hollows. Small portals lend these rooms intriguing geometry and cast interesting shadows and light. The bare walls and simple decoration complement the room's spare architecture and enhance its rustic quality.

OPPOSITE: *Each region in the Mediterranean seems to have its own heritage of ceramic tile composition and design. Tiles are used to insulate as well as brighten a room and are often employed to cover entire walls, floors, and ceilings. Bright green and blue tiles dress the walls of this Sicilian bedroom and frame frescoes of fruit-tree topiaries.*

ABOVE: *A mosaic of different tile patterns can create a wonderful effect in the bathroom. Here, assorted tiles conform to an overall design of arabesques and other Islamic motifs, all with subtle color variations.*

A B O V E : *Less is often more: few design elements are needed to enhance the natural beauty of the Mediterranean coastline. This deck has a minimal design that emphasizes the grandeur of the setting. The deck shares the weathered gray countenance of the landscape and has no balustrades or other ornamentation that might lessen the impact of the vast horizon.*

CHAPTER ONE
ARCHITECTURAL DETAILS

The span of vernacular architecture in the Mediterranean portrays the geographical and cultural diversity of the region. Nevertheless, a common sensibility can be derived from the region's disparate architecture, from the simple stone *cortijos* in the Andalusian countryside to the whitewashed domes of the Tunisian *koubba*; the rustic, rubble-stone pied-à-terre in the south of France; the solitary and majestic *casa colonica* in Italy; and the cascading, sugar-cube pile of the Greek *horta*.

The common thread is an emphasis on nature. Mediterranean homes are built from natural materials and designed to look like organic structures. Use of local materials allows the Mediterranean house to blend with its surroundings. Like nature, the home impresses with subtle variations of light, color, and texture. These elements come together in a style that is renowned for simplicity, practicality, and understated elegance.

Nature is evident in every aspect of the home, both inside and out. Houses seem to grow right from the earth, the walls jutting from the ground like rock formations. Mediterranean architecture is remarkably simple. The rugged traditional farmhouses found along the southern coasts of Spain, Italy, and France are often built of colorful local stone or stucco and have pitched roofs covered in terra-cotta tiles. Masonry is a time-honored tradition, and these dwellings seem as solid and durable as the land itself. Windows are small and walls are often up to three feet (91cm) thick, which helps insulate the house from the extreme heat of the sun. Architectural details such as window grates and balustrades are cast in wrought iron, which is a special trade of craftsmen throughout the region.

While the exteriors of these farmhouses have remained largely the same over the years, recent renovation trends have dramatically changed the interior architecture. Most notably, the ground-floor rooms of these houses, traditionally used as stalls for livestock, have been converted into magnificent kitchens and rooms for entertaining. The

OPPOSITE: *The Sicilian palette is a warm, soft medley of earthy browns, reds, and oranges. The sun has baked the earth for centuries, and the houses reflect the smoldering intensity of the soil. These burnt sienna walls enclose a luscious garden sanctuary and protect it from the more unruly elements of the climate.*

vaulted ceilings and tall, arched entryways of the original architecture lend these rooms a wonderful sense of space.

As the northern Mediterranean region became an increasingly popular vacation destination in the late nineteenth and early twentieth centuries, the architecture of the region became more grand and stylized. With roots in ancient Roman and Greek architecture, the classic style of the Mediterranean villa proliferated. The typical villa has a pitched, pantiled terra-cotta roof and rounded, columned archways over doors, windows, and terraces. Villas in the region are covered with stucco or *crepi*, a form of plaster with a rosy pink hue that embodies the muted, ever-changing colors of the local landscape.

The flat-roofed townhouses found along the beaches and ports of the northern Mediterranean, from Cannes and Monaco to Portofino and Capri, are often dramatically painted in intense, vibrant colors. These houses draw on nature's vibrant colors for their inspiration, from the pinks and oranges of the land to the innumerable blues of the sea and sky and the lush greens, reds, and yellows of local flora and fauna.

In the vertical villages of the Greek islands, perhaps the most emblematic of Mediterranean dwellings, houses are literally carved from the earth, set into steep volcanic rock and built one on top of another like steps. Roofs are usually flat, often providing space for a covered terrace, and windows and doors have simple wooden frames and appear to be haphazardly cut out of the plaster walls. To maximize interior space, staircases are traditionally built on the outside, which adds an interesting geometric element to architecture that is otherwise spare in detail. Rough-hewn shutters and doors are made from solid timber to insulate the house from the scorching sun.

Again the colors of the architecture are drawn from the surrounding nature, where the vibrant blues of the sky and sea boldly contrast with brilliant white cliffs and beaches. The doors and shutters of a classic Greek island retreat are painted azure blue, while rough plaster walls are lime-washed a brilliant white each year to approximate nature's

dazzling effect. The boldness of this color scheme is especially appropriate given the intense effect of the sun, which would tend to wash out more subtle color variations, and contrasts nicely with the simplicity of the cubic architecture.

In Morocco, Tunisia, and other parts of northern Africa, the sun-baked hues and varied textures of the earth are directly reflected in the architecture. Houses seem to spring from the rugged terrain of African deserts and mountains. Exterior walls are typically made of clay in rich shades of ocher, umber, terra-cotta, and sienna, depending on the color of the local soil. While houses can be quite simple, with flat roofs and ponderous, thick walls, the spread of Islam has endowed much of the region with an intricate and highly original architecture. The military successes of the Moorish Empire were largely responsible for the proliferation of this ornate style. As the Moors made their way across northern Africa and into Spain and Sicily, they brought this architectural style with them.

Subsequently, many of the region's most magnificent houses have a distinctly Persian look. This mosque-inspired architecture is most notably characterized by domed roofs, elaborate keyhole archways, arabesque decorative motifs, and intricate mosaics and tile work. Ceramic tiles are an integral facet of the architectural style and often cover entire walls and floors of kitchens, bathrooms, and formal sitting rooms, as well as fountains and interior courtyards.

ABOVE: *The Mediterranean is a trove of historic ruins and artifacts, and the countryside is littered with the remains of fallen kingdoms and empires. History and the inexorable passage of time are palpable in the region's infinite crumbling monuments.*

ABOVE: *The tidy Greek fishing village of Kastellórizon blends traditional design elements with contemporary sensibilities. The white walls, brightly painted shutters, and geometric configuration of the buildings show traditional Greek influence. The uniformity and order of the arrangement as a whole suggest a more contemporary civic planner at work.*

RIGHT: *Frescoes, commonly found in northern Mediterranean villas, lend a sense of grandeur and urban sophistication to the decor of rural retreats. This elegant nineteenth-century Tuscan trompe l'oeil fresco is a ghostly reminder of the grandeur of the ancient Roman empire.*

LEFT: *The color blue has countless varieties in Mediterranean design and seems to take its inspiration from the infinite shades in the sea and sky. A color wash of azure and turquoise gives this simple, arched doorway a sense of drama.*

RIGHT: *The appeal of Mediterranean homes comes in large part from the nobility of their building materials and the integrity of their construction. This house in Spain appears as solid as a fortress. Locally quarried stone was used to build the impressive staircase. The palette and texture of the house reflect the surrounding terrain and give the structure an organic quality.*

LEFT: *Few things can give a house a sense of beauty and wonder like a view of the sea. **This spacious house on the Greek island of Corfu is perched high above the water and has several terraces with astounding views.***

ABOVE: *Moroccan architecture demonstrates a profound Moorish influence. The balconies and terraces of this house in Asilah are whitewashed and lined with decorative corrugations. The arabesque archways and domed roofs also suggest the impact of Moorish design.*

ABOVE: *The houses along the shore of the Aegean Sea are blessed with spectacular views. The Greeks know the value of such blessings and take full advantage by creating splendid outdoor spaces. This house has a generously sized stone terrace that provides a stunning, unimpeded view.*

ABOVE: *Houses in the Mediterranean reflect the vibrant hues of sea and sky through their color-washed walls and bold accessories. The clean curves and sharp angles of this home in Santonini, Greece, mark it as a contemporary building, but the azure and white color scheme is traditional.*

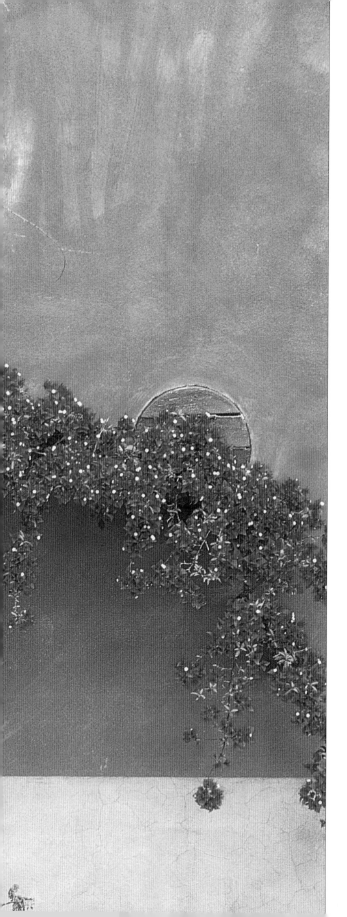

LEFT: *Flowers are a vital element of all outdoor spaces and add vivid color and soft texture to terrace architecture. Here, a thriving bougainvillea has been trained to cascade over a doorway. The sprawling nature of the flowering vines gives the architecture an organic sense of life and movement.*

ABOVE: *Things seem to age more gracefully in the Mediterranean. Here, a weathered doorway and wall have taken on a rich patina that lends this townhouse in the* centro storico *of Maratea a rustic, picturesque quality.*

ABOVE: *As the thick walls and beautiful arches of this Tuscan loggia demonstrate, renovated farmhouses benefit from sturdy construction and unusual architecture. It is an odd twist of fate that moneyed urbanites are now buying and renovating the dilapidated* casa coloniche *from which poor farmers and peasants couldn't wait to escape.*

RIGHT: *Fine Persian rugs, dark wooden furnishings, and ornately designed brass decorations are common in Moroccan interior designs. This colonnaded alcove opens onto a serene interior courtyard in Marrakech. The architecture benefits from high ceilings and a graceful arched doorway.*

CHAPTER TWO

KITCHENS AND DINING AREAS

The leisure of seaside living, the delightful fresh cooking ingredients, and the gracious yet casual way of entertaining make the Mediterranean kitchen a marvel of domesticity. The best Mediterranean kitchens are as simple and unpretentious as the food that is prepared in them. Both the cuisine and the kitchen itself can afford to be minimally dressed because of the region's natural bounty of fruits, herbs, and vegetables. Open-air markets provide fresh seafood, meat, and poultry as well as bread, cheese, olives, and other regional delicacies. Unlike the baroque comfort foods served in chillier northern climes, Mediterranean meals are remarkably light, are easy to prepare, and do not require laborious hours spent in the kitchen—which is fortunate. Who wants to toil inside when the beauty of the Mediterranean lies outdoors?

Time spent in the kitchen is kept to a minimum. A typical Mediterranean day begins with a strong espresso, a native fruit such as melon, and perhaps some freshly baked bread slathered with local jam or marmalade. For lunch, the simplest and most perfect feast is a plate of buffalo milk mozzarella sprinkled with black pepper and olive oil and topped with slices of gorgeous ripe tomatoes. Dinners are just as simple and no less delicious. The freshness of seafood and produce makes grilling a favorite nightly tradition. To escape the heat of the kitchen, grills are often set up on terraces or in other outdoor areas. Rosemary branches and other fresh herbs are often thrown right on the coals for flavor as well as aroma.

Because we have grown accustomed to countertops crowded with shiny appliances, the minimal aspect of Mediterranean home design may be most apparent in the kitchen. Compared to metropolitan ideals of luxury and convenience, the Mediterranean kitchen appears wonderfully spartan. While a good gas stove is standard, cooking hearths are not uncommon and other modern appliances are rare. Their presence is hardly missed. Mediterranean living has a distinctly elemental quality that makes such modern conveniences seem unnecessary. The slow, leisurely pace of life makes the process of shopping for fresh ingredients and preparing meals as savory as the food itself.

OPPOSITE: *White interiors are common in Greece and the southern Mediterranean. Besides being visually clean and uncluttered, monochromatic white rooms have a soothing effect and convey a sense of cool repose. Here, whitewashed walls and a pale terra-cotta floor look especially inviting as a welcome retreat from the harsh midday sun.*

The minimal aspect of the Mediterranean kitchen creates a well-defined sense of space and order. It often feels as if history itself has reduced the kitchen to its most essential elements: an array of wooden spoons and ladles, a marble cutting board, a large stone wash basin, copper pots, and locally made ceramic bowls. These implements give the kitchen a timeless quality as well as a strong sense of texture.

As in the other rooms of the Mediterranean home, the decor of the kitchen and dining area reflects local colors and textures. Floors are typically covered with terra-cotta or ceramic tiles, and stone or plaster walls are often color washed or dyed with natural pigments.

While alfresco dining is the preferred daily ritual, interior dining areas are nevertheless required to combat the midday sun and hot African winds. Whether an extension of the kitchen or its own separate room, the dining area is most notably marked by a generously proportioned wooden table and an assortment of simple, comfortable chairs. Entertaining friends and family members is a cherished part of life, and the dining table is the most obvious symbol of hospitality in the Mediterranean. While gatherings are remarkably informal, a good solid table goes far in bringing together a party of friends.

A B O V E : *Spain has a long tradition of decorating with ceramic tiles. In this kitchen, rustic tiles in a classic pattern are used to cover the walls and flue in a wholly contemporary manner. Modern appliances and a ceiling fan contrast beautifully with the traditional furnishings and terra-cotta floor.*

A B O V E : *This renovated farmhouse in Portugal retains its nineteenth-century charm. The integrity of the architecture is obvious in the thick walls and small window openings. A granite table and counters were added to complement the exposed stone walls. This kitchen looks much as it did a century ago.*

LEFT: *One could argue that the Mediterranean is most remarkable for its evocative infusions of color and light, which can transform the commonplace into the stuff of art. A bowl of lemons becomes a striking still life in Marrakech, where the color blue has infinite permutations.*

OPPOSITE: *An assortment of ceramic tiles can be used to create a cohesive design. The walls of this Majorcan kitchen are covered with tiles in a variety of patterns, yet the blue and white palette creates a sense of harmony in the space. The china and glass-ware continue the color scheme that serves to unify the room's decor.*

OPPOSITE: *Majorcan interiors have an organic, sculptural quality, as if the spaces were carved out of the earth. Shelves, cupboards, and windowsills are built into the walls, given a rough coat of plaster, and whitewashed. The integration of these architectural elements maximizes space and minimizes clutter.*

ABOVE, LEFT: *A stone basin in the kitchen is a perfect place to wash freshly picked vegetables and herbs. A spigot made from a simple, bent copper pipe sticking out of the wall gives this sink an especially rustic appearance.*

ABOVE, RIGHT: *The beauty of the Mediterranean kitchen, like the food, lies in its simplicity. Mediterranean recipes are generally uncomplicated, relying on fresh meats and produce rather than rich sauces and dressings, so cooking is more of a cherished pastime than a laborious chore. This is evident in kitchen design, where rows of gleaming appliances are distinctly absent.*

OPPOSITE: *Mediterranean interiors have a certain ad hoc charm. This Spanish dining room features a set of mismatched chairs that happen to go together remarkably well. A gingham tablecloth, a whimsical collection of blue and white china, and a display of breadboards and wooden utensils convey the relaxed nature of country design.*

ABOVE: *The French country kitchen is remarkable for its rustic charm. A yawning, open hearth is usually the centerpiece of the room, and the dining table is the most important furnishing. A weathered plank table sets the tone for this kitchen and is well matched with the rush chairs that surround it and the wicker baskets hanging overhead.*

ABOVE: *The best country kitchens have an earthy, old-world quality that evokes a sense of history. Like other aspects of the Mediterranean lifestyle, the kitchen transports us to a simpler time and place. Original architectural elements like these exposed, rough-cut ceiling beams and yellow plaster walls create a relaxed, comfortable setting.*

ABOVE: *This kitchen couples smooth and rough surfaces, and the juxtaposition brings out the tactile quality of both. Shiny green and pink ceramic tiles form a striking backsplash, while rough terra-cotta tiles cover the floor and a coarse layer of stucco lines the walls. Clear glass jars of pasta and other staples make a good display in the kitchen and convey the rustic nature of Mediterranean life.*

LEFT: *The houses in the countryside of Provence are remarkable for their relaxed, rustic style and eclectic design sensibility. This comfortable dining room features a tree-trunk table surrounded by antique garden chairs. The walls have a distempered finish, and the Provençal carpet has a simple, elegant weave that suits the rough-hewn wood plank floor exceptionally well.*

ABOVE: *When decorating a small room, pay special attention to the details. A few
fine furnishings, a pleasing color scheme, and some original architectural features can
have a dramatic effect. The soft, uneven finish of the walls in this dining room creates a
warm glow that illuminates the table setting. A simple, light tablecloth, matching blue
china, and some fresh flowers and produce complete the room.*

ABOVE: *In Morocco, outdoor retreats are often as luxurious and comfortable as indoor living rooms. A finely carved table, upholstered chairs, and a woven rug furnish this covered terrace. Thick, durable cotton curtains can be drawn to shield the terrace from stifling hot winds or tied back to allow cooling breezes to circulate.*

RIGHT: *On the island of Serifos in the Greek Cyclades, table settings often appear like still lifes. Color is a powerful design element in the Mediterranean, and is often inspired by the vibrant hues of nature's bounty. Here, a bright blue cotton tablecloth and an aqua tape-seat chair accentuate the crimson insides of a sliced prickly pear and a pitcher of brilliant magenta bougainvillea.*

ABOVE: *The terrain of the northern African coastline is vast and diverse. This terrace garden is surrounded by thick vegetation that shields the house from hot sirocco winds. As the chairs suggest, dark woods are common in the region. Interior and exterior walls are often painted in burnt sienna or rusty red.*

LEFT: *The northern African palette reflects the passionate hues of the local soil. The walls of this terrace have a rich, evocative patina indicative of regular exposure to extreme elements of sun, sea, and wind. Dark wooden furnishings and a batik tablecloth complement the architectural setting perfectly.*

CHAPTER THREE
INTERIOR LIVING SPACES

The relaxed southern European lifestyle and the sense of retreat that is brought to these shores from abroad each summer lend a remarkably informal air to Mediterranean living spaces. Life there is about comfort and relaxation, and every aspect of interior design in the region supports that notion. Mediterranean homes have a remarkably lived-in quality, and each furnishing seems to invite a moment's perfect repose: a window cushion for the morning's solitary espresso, a cozy couch for siesta, and a grouping of worn armchairs for sipping Italian grappa, Greek ouzo, or Spanish sangria, smoking Tunisian narghiles, and talking among family and friends late into the night.

One of the most evocative qualities of the Mediterranean is its sense of timelessness, and interior living spaces reflect this quality. Decorating trends and fashions hold no sway. Interior design, in fact, is rarely achieved by design at all. Furnishings are chosen for their individual function or beauty, and not necessarily for how they might come together in a design scheme. The overall effect—that of a collection of beautiful found objects—is a deeply personal expression, one rich with favorite anecdotes of distant travel and local haggling, accidental discovery and fortunate happenstance.

Much of the allure of Mediterranean living lies in the beauty of nature and the surrounding landscape. Mediterranean homes are designed with this in mind, and living spaces often blur the distinction between interior and exterior space and architecture. To achieve this effect, natural colors and materials are used on floors and walls. Interior walls are made with the same local materials and techniques used to construct the house's facade and are often left bare or are roughly plastered and whitewashed. Walls can also be painted with natural pigments or given a more traditional color wash, which has a matte, chalky texture and can be applied in subtle color variations. Floors are stone or wood or are covered with terra-cotta or ceramic tiles. Carpeting is seldom used; floors are usually left bare or covered with throw rugs. Window and door architraves, including the stone lintels and terra-cotta moldings that are an intrinsic feature of a house's exterior, are often left exposed and unfinished inside.

Windows and doors are treated less as barriers to the elements than as open thresholds. Views of astounding land- and seascapes are

OPPOSITE: *What's old is what's new. The best contemporary designs often do not stray far from the past. Original architectural detail, muted colors, and simple yet timeless furnishings give this Marrakech house a feeling of turn-of-the-century dignity.*

not uncommon, of course, but Mediterranean living rooms embrace more sublime natural settings as well. Salons, sitting rooms, libraries, and other interior gathering places usually offer uninhibited access to gardens or outdoor terraces. It is not necessary to dress windows, but when drapery is used, it is rendered simply in light fabrics that catch the breeze. To maximize air circulation and to bring the outside in, doors and windows are often left wide open. Potted plants are found everywhere and help to promote the illusion of being outdoors.

Fussy, formal decors do not exist in the Mediterranean. Living spaces are made for lounging, and soft, comfortable furnishings are of paramount importance. Couches and upholstered chairs are covered in tough, durable fabrics and arranged in informal clusters. Cushions are often made to cover the hard surfaces of rustic wood furniture or wrought-iron garden pieces. Mediterranean textiles are famous the world over and lend softness and a strong sense of color and texture to living spaces. Provençal cotton fabrics in bright, vivid floral and paisley patterns are commonly used to upholster chairs and couches and quickly brighten a room. The rich embroideries of Morocco and northern Africa and the flat-weaves of Turkey are also prevalent and are used throughout the region as wall hangings, cushions, and throws.

A strong aesthetic is apparent throughout the Mediterranean in decorative collections and displays. The sea itself is perhaps the most emblematic decorative motif, and fish, shells, boats, and other nautical themes are commonly displayed. Remnants of history are another powerful decorative element. Fragments of ancient sculpture and pottery, old coins, and other archaeological finds are common collectibles. Locally produced crafts such as wood carvings, baskets, mosaics, and ceramics are ubiquitous and convey the beautiful simplicity of Mediterranean life.

OPPOSITE: *The influence of color cannot be overemphasized in Mediterranean design. This Moroccan sitting room is decorated with a warm rainbow of yellows, oranges, and reds. Each shade is just slightly different so that the theme is maintained, but a subtle, nuanced effect is achieved.*

ABOVE: *Ribbon and bead curtains can be used to provide shade for interior spaces while still allowing air to circulate. The free-flowing curtains offer many decorative possibilities and serve to deter insects, which are dissuaded from entering by the apparent barrier and its constant movement. These curtains are often made of strips of fabric, colorful ribbons, or knotted rope or string. More inspired decorators may use strings of beads or shells.*

ABOVE, LEFT: *Provençal interiors typically bring together modest, simple country aesthetics with more sophisticated design influences. The result is a wonderful juxtaposition of styles and sensibilities. This salon is furnished with richly embroidered curtains and period antiques that suggest an urban influence, yet overall the room retains the understated charm of a country retreat.*

ABOVE, RIGHT: *Vibrant color pervades Moroccan interiors. Wall pigments often assume nearly neon hues, and embroidered fabrics can be just as electric. In any other setting, orange, pink, and blue might clash, but here they seem to emphasize the energy and vitality of the culture as well as the bold contrasts of the landscape.*

RIGHT:

Mediterraneans spend as much time as possible outside, so it is not surprising that the terrace is often the most popular room of the house. That is certainly the case in this northern African bungalow, where thick vegetation creeps up the walls, providing privacy and a natural buffer from hot sirocco winds.

LEFT: *This living room on the Spanish island of Ibiza has a distinctly Moorish flavor. From the elaborate brass lanterns hanging from the ceiling to the intricately decorated side table and oil lamp, all the furnishings conform to a Persian aesthetic brought to the island centuries ago. The plush sofas and low, dark wooden tables also have origins in Eastern design.*

ABOVE: *Round, smooth stones and pebbles can be found along rivers and beaches throughout the Mediterranean and are often used in house construction. In Provence, these floors are closely packed, with little space between the individual stones. The highly textured cobblestone effect is typically offset by smooth tiled pathways. This bedroom in a home in the town of Tarascon is further softened by a velvety red wall finish.*

OPPOSITE: *Simple design, close attention to detail, and exquisite craftsmanship are hallmarks of the Mediterranean home. The sturdy windows and doors of this northern Italian cottage help make a modest dwelling into a special retreat.*

RIGHT: *French country style is marked by comfort and simple elegance. This living room has a relaxed country sensibility that is enhanced by a few urban touches. The soft, comfortable sofa is placed under a window that allows in plenty of warm sun and cool breezes, making it the perfect spot for a nap.*

LEFT, TOP:

Contemporary Mediterranean design often reflects traditional motifs. The bedroom in this Moroccan-style house has a decidedly modern design, but the Persian influence is nevertheless clear. While the platform bed has a sleek, contemporary quality, the arabesque headboard stenciled on the wall reveals the designer's cultural inspiration.

LEFT, BOTTOM:

Moroccan interiors fuse African and Middle Eastern design influences. In this sitting room in Marrakech, the design and coloration of the pillows reflect African design, while the kilim rug suggests a distinctly Eastern influence.

ABOVE: *Mediterranean interiors have simple, modest furnishings that reflect local craftsmanship. The iron and wood furniture in this living room has a rustic quality that helps create a sense of put-your-feet-up comfort and relaxation. The ceramic pitcher and bowls were fired in a nearby kiln.*

OPPOSITE: *On the Spanish island of Mallorca, traditional interiors tend to appear like the carved-out hollows of a grotto. Walls are unevenly plastered and whitewashed and often have shelves, hearths, and benches molded into them. Beautiful decorative displays can be made out of everyday tools and implements, as this collection of locally blown glass bottles suggests.*

ABOVE: *The Greek island of Serifos remains largely untouched by modern development, and the architecture there appears today much as it did several centuries ago. Walls are thick and unevenly plastered and whitewashed. Floors are cast in stone, and ceilings are lined with rough-hewn timber. Hearths, which are often still used for cooking, are carved directly into the walls.*

LEFT, TOP: *Doors and windows are left open in Greece in the early morning and late afternoon to allow cool breezes to flow through the house. Shutters are drawn in the afternoon to protect against the wilting heat. Whitewashed walls are typically offset by azure blue windows and doors.*

LEFT, BOTTOM: *In northern Africa, Moorish customs have greatly influenced the design heritage. Sitting and dining areas are often furnished with ottomans or low-slung chairs situated around a table. Design embellishments tend to be more ornate, as this intricate latticework suggests.*

RIGHT: *Life in the Mediterranean is marked by a confluence of differing cultures. Thousands of years of trade, migration, and invasion have transformed the region and made it a true melting pot of peoples and traditions. A collection of signs and advertisements in many native tongues, therefore, has a special significance and suggests the rich diversity in the Mediterranean.*

CHAPTER FOUR
BEDROOMS AND BATHS

In this land of the siesta, a relentless sun, and infernal sirocco winds, the best thing that can be said of a Mediterranean bedroom is that it offers a sense of cool, dark repose. Heat and sunlight permeate life throughout the region, and a respite from the elements can seem a luxury. To achieve a suitably cool, cavernous effect, slatted shutters are kept closed during the day, diffusing the light while still allowing sea breezes to circulate.

A sanctuary of sorts, the bedroom has a softer look than other rooms in the house, and textiles tend to play a larger role in the decor. The bed is the focus of the room, of course, and is often draped with a gauzy canopy or crowned with a sheer cotton corona. The drapery affords protection from mosquitoes while allowing air to circulate, but it can also create a dramatic visual effect. Cotton sheets and bedspreads are soothing and breathe easily on hot summer nights.

To diffuse strong midday light, windows may be treated with curtains or thin drapes. Simplicity is still the rule, however. Window treatments are light and never fussy. Fine cotton embroidery or filmy muslin fabrics hang breezily from plain wooden or metal poles. These treatments filter harsh light and welcome cooling gusts.

Throw rugs offer another softening effect in the bedroom. While floors are usually tile or hardwood, throw rugs bring color and comforting texture to the bedroom. Flat-weaves, embroidered cotton throws, and sisal and other vegetable-fiber carpets are common floor coverings throughout the Mediterranean and reflect the melding of several different traditions. While some throws are intricately designed and lend an air of sophistication, others are woven in a single bright color that is just as effective.

Like the bedroom, the Mediterranean bathroom is a place of shadowy retreat. With mesmerizing sea views never far from sight, water is a way of life and an evocative design motif. Nowhere is this theme more evident than in the bath, where the soothing, recuperative qualities of water can best be appreciated. The best bathrooms are equipped with decadently large tubs. Submerged in cool spring-water and quiet midday darkness, one feels very much in tune with the eternal rhythm of this place, the perpetual ebb and flow of Mediterranean life.

OPPOSITE: *Contrasting textures are a recurring theme in Mediterranean interiors. Here, the smooth sheen of highly polished terra-cotta floor tiles contrasts with the matte whitewashed walls and filmy muslin bed curtains. The room has an elegant, tactile quality that elicits a physical as well as an emotional response.*

Ceramic tiles are used throughout the home but seem essential within the aqueous realm of the bathroom. Shiny and cool to the touch, ceramic tiles have a fluid quality that helps convey this room's water theme. Spanish and Italian tiles tend to be bright and colorful and often have floral motifs. In northern Africa, where Moorish influence is still strong, tile work usually has a more intricate, geometric aspect, and elaborate mosaics are common.

Several different tile patterns can be used simultaneously in the bathroom to create a sophisticated look. For example, a backsplash or tub surround of intricate Islamic tiles can be edged with plain tiles in matching hues that have been set into a simple geometric pattern. Tiled floors and walls often have a contrasting tile border, and basins, showers, and vanities can have yet another motif. Borders and accents usually reflect a color or pattern in the wall or floor and serve to complete the room's visual effect.

ABOVE: *Mediterranean interiors demonstrate a remarkable economy of design. A few good pieces can make a room. Here, a highly polished dresser, a two-tone wicker chair, and a soft bed are all that is needed to complete the bedroom with style and elegance. The walls have a warm sienna finish that complements the rough terra-cotta floor wonderfully.*

OPPOSITE: *This Moroccan-style bathroom on the island of Ibiza demonstrates the vast potential of designing with ceramic tiles. Various tile colors and patterns can be used together to create wonderful, vivid interiors. Bold geometric shapes can be mixed with floral motifs as well as more complex designs that will come together like a rich, textured tapestry.*

ABOVE, LEFT: *Pale green shutters faded by the sun turn this peaceful bedroom into a cool sanctuary in the heat of the day. A simple quilt, made from squares of various bold and natural hues, dresses the comfortable bed and provides the only color in this all-white room.*

ABOVE, RIGHT: *Bigger isn't always better, and small rooms can certainly be made beautiful. This bedroom has several quirky architectural features that are indicative of Mediterranean design: the rounded blue fireplace in the corner, the asymmetrical window treatment, and the grooved ceiling.*

*Mediterranean blue
can be used both
indoors and out to
great effect. Inside,
as in this bedroom in
Asilah, Morocco, the
color blue has a cool,
soothing quality.
White is the perfect
complement, of
course, as these bed
linens demonstrate.
Each color seems to
illuminate and
energize the other.*

LEFT: *A wall of diaphanous fabric can be used to distinguish a space and instill a sense of allure and romance. This modest bedroom in Ibiza is enclosed in muslin drapes, allowing air to circulate while creating a dramatic proscenium for the platform bed.*

OPPOSITE: *This contemporary home has an austere appearance that reflects the flavor of Mediterranean style. The walls, windows, and doors have no moldings or other embellishments that might take away from the strong linear composition of the design. The rough walls are painted a neutral tone that enhances the effect.*

ABOVE: *Thick stone walls help to keep this bedroom cool in summer and warm in winter. The texture of the walls also brings an interesting design element to the room. A translucent muslin canopy hangs over the bed and serves to protect against mosquitoes while allowing cool breezes to pass.*

RIGHT: *After a morning spent in the sun sailing, hiking, or lying on the beach, the afternoon siesta is best enjoyed in darkness. This bedroom in a home on the Spanish coastline is well equipped for the siesta: damask bed linens, a high peaked ceiling, and a tile floor promise a comfortable escape from the sun. Most importantly, the shuttered windows and doors shield the bedroom from the sun's intensity.*

ABOVE: *Old-world allure can be achieved in a variety of ways. The architectural elements, as well as the decor of this Moroccan bedroom, seem well suited for Lawrence of Arabia. Molded high ceilings, elaborate wall sconces, and a fanciful chandelier lend the room a colonial, turn-of-the-century aspect that is complemented by the bed linens and other furnishings.*

ABOVE: *White-on-white interiors can have an especially soothing effect in Mediterranean climates. This bedroom is minimally decorated, yet the sumptuous bed makes the room very appealing. The simple wrought-iron canopy is draped in lightweight cotton. The pillow shams and sheets are classic white damask and prove that fine bed linens are worth the significant investment.*

ABOVE: *Vast space and beautiful colonnaded archways give this bathroom a sense of imperial luxury. The bathroom in this converted farmhouse was formerly an open terrace, and the room benefits greatly from the original architecture. Not all houses can afford such large bathrooms, but the Mediterranean predilection for comfort and uncluttered space often permits a decadent retreat for long afternoon baths.*

ABOVE: *This oversize bathroom is well equipped with modern amenities such as electric lighting, yet maintains its old-world elegance and charm. A shoulder-high copper tub is a rare treat, but one can only imagine the luxury of a roaring fire in the hearth. The tub is outfitted with two swan's head water spouts that add to the allure.*

ABOVE, LEFT: *Moorish courtyards and gardens were traditionally designed as peaceful retreats from the outside world. Water and shade have always played an important role in these soothing settings. Interior courtyards are often lined with tile and include a pool or fountain. This open-air bath pavilion in Marrakech provides shade from the sun and is often used for refreshment during the afternoon siesta.*

ABOVE, RIGHT: *Interesting architecture is as important inside as it is out. Strong shapes create a sense of drama in this bathroom. The two narrow rectangular windows make a strong visual statement within the soft curve of the arch and above the rounded sink, lending an evocative, sculptural quality to the interior architecture.*

ABOVE: *Moorish influence reveals itself in many different styles of design. The sculpted, warmly hued walls of this bathroom in Ibiza imbue the room with a remarkable serenity. The hanging lantern adds to the effect by radiating a muted, dappled light. Overall, the room has a soft, tranquil quality that reflects the Islamic propensity for calm, peaceful settings.*

CHAPTER FIVE

OUTDOOR RETREATS

Mediterranean life revolves around the outdoors. Whether hiking, sailing, swimming, or just sunning and relaxing on a beach, one cannot resist the temptation to be outside. The sun, sea, and fresh air have a therapeutic effect on the body and soul and instill a wonderful sense of well-being.

As we have seen, the beauty of the natural surroundings is incorporated into the design of the Mediterranean house. Interior spaces open to breathtaking views of land and sea and blur the distinction between inside and out. A broad panorama or a simple garden vista is the most remarkable aspect of many beautiful interiors.

Nevertheless, the desire to be outside is strong, and courtyards, terraces, and other outdoor retreats prove to be the most treasured "rooms" of the house. After a long morning in the sun and sea and a soporific lunch of fresh seafood, fruit, and wine, the shade of a vine-covered pergola or the cool dampness of a fountain courtyard makes for a pleasant siesta. Alfresco dining is the preferred way to entertain, and family and friends will congregate around an outdoor dining table for hours at a time. To make this sort of entertaining feasible, the outdoor retreat must be a shaded place that is accessible at all times of the day. The midday sun can be fierce, so the first priority is to provide protection from direct sunlight.

Terraces and garden patios are common among the farmhouses and cloistered homes found along the southern European coastline. They are situated close to the house and, when well positioned, are sheltered from strong winds. Terraces are covered by lean-to roofs that extend from the house and are constructed of cane, bamboo, or heavier timber. Iron frames are draped in canvas to make attractive awnings over a terrace area. Pergolas offer another means of escape from the sun and emit wonderful fragrances as well. Bougainvillea, rose, and honeysuckle are especially pretty and thrive in the balmy Mediterranean climate. Like roofed terraces, pergolas provide protection from the sun without obstructing the summer breeze or concealing views of the landscape.

OPPOSITE: *Along Italy's Amalfi Coast, the time-worn facade of this villa creates a dramatic backdrop for a candlelit alfresco meal in a sheltered interior courtyard. The architecture has an integrity of design and construction that is typical of Mediterranean houses. While the design is simple and elegant, with windows and doors neatly cut out of the walls, the building has a remarkable solidity that gives it a sense of timelessness.*

Larger houses are often arranged around interior courtyards. With origins in Moorish and Roman architecture as well as in the age-old design of coastal fortifications, courtyards provide an escape from the often harsh elements: their high surrounding walls not only provide shade but also serve to block hot, dry winds. Fountains and shady trees are frequently part of the design as well.

Outdoor retreats unify the various elements of the Mediterranean home, bringing together nature, architecture, and interior design. As an extension of both the external architecture and the interior decor, outdoor spaces fuse aspects of each. Retaining walls, floors, and paths are rendered in the same building materials as the house. Stone, brick, distempered stucco, whitewashed plaster, and even ceramic tiles are commonly used for terrace and courtyard walls. Terra-cotta tiles, bricks, stone, and slate can be used inside and out.

Interior design concepts are applicable to outdoor furnishings as well. Comfort is a primary concern, although outdoor furniture must also be weather-resistant. The pleasure of alfresco dining makes an outdoor dining table a must. While designs vary, the table must be large enough to seat family and friends. A simple wooden farm table can be as elegant as an elaborately crafted mosaic table. Other furniture includes a wide assortment of lounge chairs and chaises. Outdoor chairs are typically made of wood or wrought iron and covered with brightly colored cushions. A whimsical array of terra-cotta and ceramic urns and flowerpots completes the outdoor space.

ABOVE: *Mediterranean houses are typically flanked by numerous terraces, and rooms often open onto patio gardens. French doors with bright red shutters lead from this bedroom to a lush, secluded terrace. This cloistered space along the Spanish coast can be a quiet haven for enjoying the morning coffee or a cool respite from the afternoon sun.*

OPPOSITE: *This portico has a wonderfully lyric design that lends the otherwise heavy stone architecture a sense of whimsy and lightness. Its organic quality is enhanced by the reed-lined roof and the bougainvillea climbing the walls.*

OPPOSITE: *No Mediterranean terrace or patio is complete without an array of potted flowers and plants. Terra-cotta pots come in a variety of shapes and sizes and weather attractively to a soft, mellow tone. This row of geraniums adds grandeur to the staircase, highlighting the building's architecture and contributing a splash of color to the muted palette.*

RIGHT: *This bedroom loggia represents the perfect union of nature and design. The architecture blends seamlessly with its natural setting, as flowering vines creep along aggregate stone walls and a rough-hewn timber balcony.*

OPPOSITE: *Formality has no place in Mediterranean design. Ad hoc elegance is the rule and not the exception. Here, a canvas awning is casually draped between two trees to provide shade on the terrace and create a relaxing, breezy retreat from the sun.*

ABOVE: *The late-afternoon sun falls gently on this covered terrace on the island of Corfu, creating a wonderful spot from which to view the comings and goings of sailboats in the distance. Proportions are an important design consideration: tall pillars and a broad stone facade lend a stately presence to this house.*

ABOVE: *The Spanish countryside is hot and dry during the summer, which makes this lush oasis especially alluring. The palette of the house and pool surround melds with the setting perfectly. Umber walls and terra-cotta tiles reflect the colors of the arid, rocky terrain in the distance, while the green pool looks cool and shadowy, like the surrounding gardens.*

OPPOSITE: *This poolside table for two is especially inviting with the French Pyrenees in the background, but the design elements certainly add to the romantic ambience. Bright flowers, ripe fruit, and dark red wine look appetizing against the cool blue of the tablecloth. The pool and the weathered stone terrace have a picturesque quality that suits the surrounding wilderness.*

LEFT: *Nature works remarkably well in Mediterranean architecture. This Spanish pergola faces an interior courtyard and demonstrates how beautifully nature can be integrated into design. The dappled shade of a pergola is one of the most refreshing places to while away the afternoon siesta.*

ABOVE: *Mediterranean gardens often make lush sanctuaries for alfresco dining. While this outdoor setting has tremendous natural beauty, the table setting complements the surroundings admirably. The brightly printed cotton table linens and fresh fruit bring out the ripe colors in the garden.*

INDEX

PHOTO CREDITS